STAND UP: Bullying Prevention

GROUP BULLYING
EXCLUSION AND GANGING UP

Addy Ferguson

PowerKiDS press.

New York

Published in 2013 by The Rosen Publishing Group, Inc.
29 East 21st Street, New York, NY 10010

First Edition

Editor: Jennifer Way
Book Design: Erica Clendening and Colleen Bialecki

Photo Credits: Cover Altrendo Images/Getty Images; pp. 5–6 SW Productions/Photodisc/Getty Images; p. 7 Hemera/Thinkstock; p. 8 iStockphoto/Thinkstock; p. 9 O Driscoll Imaging/Shutterstock.com; p. 11 Cultura/Nancy Honey/StockImage/Getty Images; p. 12 Jupiter Images/Brand X Pictures/Getty Images; p. 13 Chris Whitehead/Digital Vision/Getty Images; p. 14 Digital Vision/Thinkstock; p. 15 Stockbyte/Getty Images; p. 16 Uppercut Images/Getty Images; p. 17 Gladskik Tatiana/Shutterstock.com; p. 18 Rayman/Digital Vision/Getty Images; p. 19 Sam Edwards/OJO Images/Getty Images; p. 20 © iStockphoto.com/iofoto; p. 21 Dirk Anschutz/Stone/Getty Images; p. 22 © iStockphoto.com/Adam Kazmierski.

Library of Congress Cataloging-in-Publication Data

Ferguson, Addy.
 Group bullying : exclusion and ganging up / by Addy Ferguson. — 1st ed.
     p. cm. — (Stand up : bullying prevention)
 Includes index.
 ISBN 978-1-4488-9669-1 (library binding) — ISBN 978-1-4488-9796-4 (pbk.) —
 ISBN 978-1-4488-9797-1 (6-pack)
 1. Bullying—Juvenile literature. 2. Bullying—Prevention—Juvenile literature. 3. Self-esteem—Juvenile literature. I. Title.
 BF637.B85F468 2013
 302.34'3—dc23
                                     2012026339
Manufactured in the United States of America

CPSIA Compliance Information: Batch #W13PK4: For Further Information contact Rosen Publishing, New York, New York at 1-800-237-9932

Contents

What Is Bullying?

Have you ever been bullied? Have you known someone who has been bullied? If you have, then you know that bullying is **aggressive** behavior in which one person threatens or hurts another person, either **physically** or **verbally**, or **excludes** someone from a group. This behavior happens more than once and does not stop when the victim tells the bully to stop.

This book will take a look at group bullying. This is the type of bullying in which a group of people bullies another person by excluding or ganging up on their victim.

Group bullying can take different forms. The group might gang up on a target physically, they may all taunt him, or they may all exclude him.

Types of Bullies

There are many kinds of bullying, all of which can be done by one person or by a group. Verbal bullying happens when a person or group uses words to hurt their victim. They could say things that scare the other person, say they will hurt another person, or spread **rumors**.

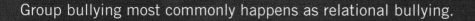

Group bullying most commonly happens as relational bullying.

Physical bullies use their bodies to hurt another person. **Cyberbullies** use computers, cell phones, and **social-networking sites** to bully others. Some bullies get others to leave their victim out of activities or groups. This is called **relational**, or social, bullying.

Bullying Hurts!

Every kind of bullying hurts its victim. The effects can last long after the bullying stops, too. Think about how you would feel if a group of girls laughed every time you walked by, made fun of your clothes, or would not let you play with them.

Kids who are being bullied may start to spend more time alone. This can make depression and loneliness feel much worse, though.

Soon other people might join in the bullying. You then start spending your recess sitting alone, hoping nobody notices you. It might make you feel **depressed** or angry. You might start worrying about what you are wearing or what people think of you. These feelings are the outcome of bullying.

What Is a Clique?

You likely have seen groups of girls or boys who spend a lot of time together in the halls, at lunch, or at recess. Sometimes these groups are open to others joining their activities. Other times they are not. A group that does not readily let outside people in is called a **clique**. Cliques often have a leader, a second in command, and others who are also eager to please and fit in with the group.

Cliques can use the power of numbers to tease, ignore, and otherwise bully targets outside their groups. Are there any cliques in your school?

Although many people think of cliques as groups of girls, boys form these friendship groups, too.

Cliques, Ganging Up, and Exclusion

Cliques sometimes gang up and exclude others. When a group gangs up on another person, they all take part in **humiliating**, taunting, or hurting another person. It is bad enough to have one person say mean things to you, imagine a whole group of people joining in!

Sometimes a friend may join a clique and start excluding her old friends to fit in with the new group. This kind of exclusion feels very hurtful to her old friends.

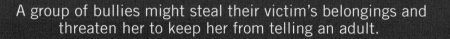

A group of bullies might steal their victim's belongings and threaten her to keep her from telling an adult.

Another way cliques can bully people is by excluding them. They send the message that their target does not measure up or is not good enough to join their group. They may say untrue things about the person, share personal information, or use other methods to embarrass and shun the person.

Walk Away, Don't Fight

When a group is ganging up on you, the best thing to do is walk away and ignore them. If you can firmly tell them to leave you alone, then do it, but you do not want to sound like you are pleading or scared. The bully wants a reaction, so ignoring his taunts sometimes ends the bullying.

It can be hard to walk away from a group that is bullying you. This keeps the group from seeing you react to them, though.

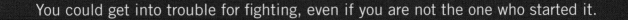

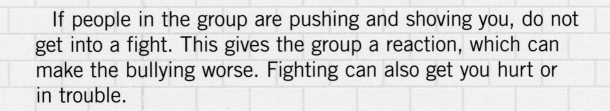

If people in the group are pushing and shoving you, do not get into a fight. This gives the group a reaction, which can make the bullying worse. Fighting can also get you hurt or in trouble.

Talk to an Adult

One of the reasons bullying is so common is that the victims do not tell anyone. They may be afraid the bullying will get worse. They might think no one can or will help them.

Many kids do not tell their parents about bullying because they do not want them to worry. It is important to talk to someone about bullying, though.

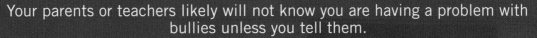

Do not keep what is happening to yourself. Tell a trusted adult, such as a parent or teacher. This person can help you feel better and can help you put a stop to the bullying. She can give you ideas on what you can do, whom to talk to, and how to deal with your feelings of anger, sadness, fear, or shame.

Building Self-Esteem

Being picked on and bullied by a group of people does not feel good. The victim may start to feel bad about herself, thinking maybe the bullies would not target her if she were not different from them.

Taking part in an activity you enjoy is a good way to improve your self-esteem.

Talking to a friend about your feelings can help you deal with the effects of bullying.

The way we feel about ourselves is called **self-esteem**. Do not let bullies hurt your self-esteem. Bullying is never the target's fault. Be true to yourself. Do not change who you are to please others. If you are feeling depressed or angry, it can help to talk with a **counselor**. A counselor can help you deal with your feelings.

Bully-Free Schools

Many schools have decided to take action against bullying. The students in the school agree to make their school a bully-free zone, where all kids can feel safe. Each student needs to speak out when he sees bullying happening. The idea is that if the whole school works together as a community, then there will be less bullying.

If there is not an antibullying program at your school, there might be a teacher who would be willing to start this kind of group. It doesn't hurt to ask!

If your school has a student government, it could get the school to put antibullying policies in place.

If your school does not have an antibullying program, you and your friends could start one. Talk to your teacher or the school's principal about your idea. Putting an end to bullying can start with one person who wants to make a change!

Everybody Deserves Respect

Whether a bully works alone or is part of a group, what he is doing is wrong. Everyone deserves to be respected.

If you or someone you know is being bullied, there are lots of resources that can help. There are websites that have more information and tips on how to stop bullying. You have the power to stop bullying at your school. Stop standing by and stand up!

Everyone is responsible for her own behavior, whether acting alone or as part of a group. You are doing the right thing when you refuse to go along with group bullying.

Glossary

aggressive (uh-GREH-siv) Ready to fight.

clique (KLIK) A small, sometimes mean group of people.

counselor (KOWN-seh-ler) Someone who talks with people about their feelings and problems.

cyberbullies (SY-ber-bu-leez) People who do hurtful or threatening things to other people using the Internet.

depressed (dih-PRESD) Having a sickness in which a person is very sad for a long time.

excludes (eks-KLOODZ) Keeps or shuts someone out.

humiliating (hyoo-MIH-lee-ayt-ing) Making someone else feel very bad about himself or herself.

physically (FIH-zih-kul-ee) Done with the body.

relational (rih-LAY-shnul) Having to do with the ties between people.

rumors (ROO-murz) Stories that are heard by people without knowing if they are true.

self-esteem (self-uh-STEEM) Happiness with oneself.

social-networking sites (soh-shul-NET-wur-king SYTS) Websites that allow members to interact.

verbally (VER-bul-ee) Done with words.

23

Index

A
activities, 7, 10

B
bully, 4, 7, 14,
    18–19, 22

C
clothes, 8
computers, 7
counselor, 19

E
effects, 8

F
feelings, 9, 17, 19

G
girls, 8, 10

H
halls, 10

K
leader, 10
lunch, 10

O
outcome, 9

S
second in
    command, 10
self-esteem, 19

Websites

Due to the changing nature of Internet links, PowerKids Press has developed an online list of websites related to the subject of this book. This site is updated regularly. Please use this link to access the list:
www.powerkidslinks.com/subp/group/